Reycraft Books
145 Huguenot Street
New Rochelle, NY 10801
Reycraftbooks.com

Reycraft Books is a trade imprint and trademark of Newmark Learning LLC.
Text © 2025 Annette Whipple
Illustration © 2025 Reycraft Books

Expert review provided by Dr. Alexandra M. Martin.

All rights reserved. No portion of this book may be reproduced, stored in a retrieval system, or transmitted in any form or by any means, electronic, mechanical, photocopying, recording, or otherwise, without written permission from the publisher. For information regarding permission, please contact info@reycraftbooks.com.

Educators and Librarians: Our books may be purchased in bulk for promotional, educational, or business use. Please contact sales@reycraftbooks.com.

The publisher does not have any control over and does not assume any responsibility for author or third-party websites or their content.

Sale of this book without a front cover or jacket may be unauthorized. If this book is coverless, it may have been reported to the publisher as "unsold or destroyed" and may have deprived the author and publisher of payment.

Library of Congress Control Number: 2024933281

Hardcover ISBN: 978-1-4788-8780-5
Paperback ISBN: 978-1-4788-8781-2

Photo Credits: Page 3B: mauritius images GmbH/Alamy; Page 4A, 5A: Stocktrek Images, Inc./Alamy; Page 7A: Ron Niebrugge/Alamy; Page 8: Zvitaliy/Alamy; Page 9A: Alberto Masnovo/Alamy; Page 10B: Danita Delimont Creative/Alamy; Page 12A, 13A: USGS/Alamy; Page 13B: USGS; Page 14: Hemis/Alamy; Page 18A, 19A: Nature Picture Library/Alamy; Page 23B: The Color Archives/Alamy; Page 23C, 27J: imageBROKER/Alamy; Page 24, Inside Back Cover: Douglas Peebles Photography/Alamy; Back Cover B: Rachel Burns; Page 27A: blickwinkel/Alamy; Page 27B: Lindsey Swierk; Page 27E: Joe Blossom/Alamy; Page 27E: Joe Blossom/Alamy; Page 27J: Avalon.red/Alamy; Page 27K: Dorling Kindersley ltd/Alamy; Page 31A: Martin Harvey/Alamy; All other images from Shutterstock and Getty Images

Illustration Credits: JuanbJuan Oliver

Author photo courtesy of Meghan Whipple.

Printed in Dongguan, China. 949559/0625/22941

10 9 8 7 6 5 4 3 2 1

First Edition Hardcover published by Reycraft Books 2025.

Reycraft Books and Newmark Learning LLC. support diversity and the First Amendment, and celebrate the right to read.

THE FLICKING TONGUE.

THE COLOR-CHANGING SKIN.

 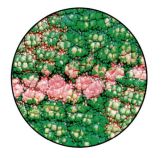

THE WATCHFUL EYES.

Lizards amaze us with their variety. Geckos, iguanas, and skinks are some of the reptiles that scientists group together and call lizards.

All of the nearly 8,000 lizard species living today are unique and remarkable.

Scales & Tails

I'm as long as a basketball hoop is high!

I'm the size of a sunflower seed!

WHAT IS A LIZARD?

male green iguana

Lizards are the most common kind of reptile. Like other reptiles, lizards have dry, scaly skin. They usually hatch from eggs.

Typically, lizards' long bodies have four legs as well as tails. Most lizards have eyelids.

Many lizards have distinct characteristics. Ridges called crests form along the backs and tails of some lizards—and sometimes on their eyelids. The crested gecko's "eyelashes" keep dust from its eyes. Some lizards have a flap of skin under their chin called a dewlap. Male green anoles extend their dewlap to show their pink necks to females.

Where do Lizards LIVE?

Lizards make their homes in a variety of habitats. Striped legless skinks slither through desert sand. Many geckos and chameleons climb high in rainforest treetops. Eastern collared lizards live among rocks and sleep under boulders. Water anoles dive in rivers, and marine iguanas swim in the ocean.

As cold-blooded creatures, lizards use their environment to change their body temperature. Some lizards bask in the sun to warm themselves. Other lizards need to prevent overheating, so desert-dwellers often dig burrows in the sand to stay cool.

Lizards who live in areas with cold winters survive with a deep rest called brumation. When their heart rate and breathing slow for a long time, it's like hibernation for cold-blooded reptiles.

Argentine black-and-white tegu

female panther chameleon

underwater marine iguana

toad-headed agama

Mexican beaded lizard

Scales & Tails

When temperatures drop, get your umbrellas handy. It'll be **raining iguanas!**

We lose our grip on branches and fall out of trees when temperatures drop below 40° Fahrenheit. After we warm up, we scurry away.

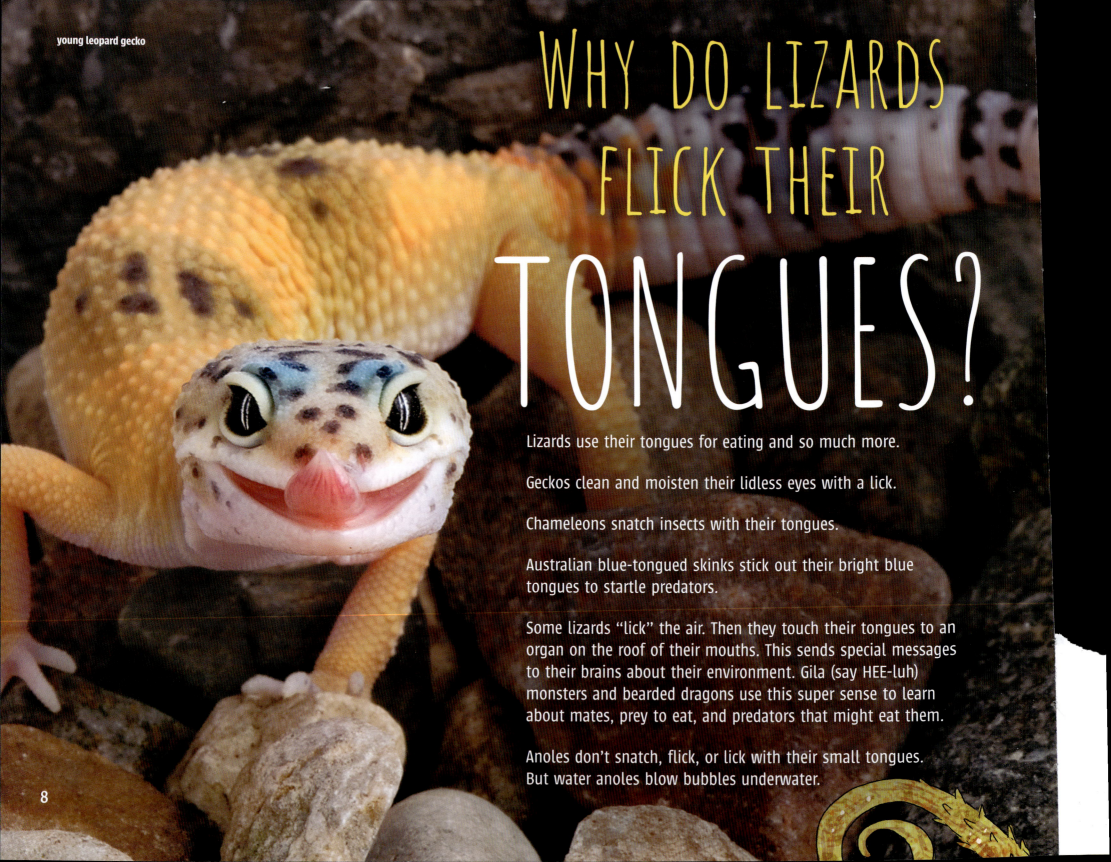

young leopard gecko

Why do lizards flick their tongues?

Lizards use their tongues for eating and so much more.

Geckos clean and moisten their lidless eyes with a lick.

Chameleons snatch insects with their tongues.

Australian blue-tongued skinks stick out their bright blue tongues to startle predators.

Some lizards "lick" the air. Then they touch their tongues to an organ on the roof of their mouths. This sends special messages to their brains about their environment. Gila (say HEE-luh) monsters and bearded dragons use this super sense to learn about mates, prey to eat, and predators that might eat them.

Anoles don't snatch, flick, or lick with their small tongues. But water anoles blow bubbles underwater.

Scales & Tails

veiled chameleon

close-up of gecko

black and white tegu lizard

pair of white-lined gecko hands

Most lizards have four legs with five clawed toes on each foot. Their toes help them in their various habitats.

Some lizards climb. Iguanas have sharp claws that help them crawl over rocks and grip tree branches. The sticky toe pads of many geckos make them incredible climbers.

Other lizards have special scales on their toes. Fringe-toed lizards dash across sand dunes and practically swim through sand to escape predators. Plumed basilisks spread their weight on their fringed toes and create air pockets under their feet. Then they race—upright—across water. Web-footed geckos' feet work like shovels. They dig fresh burrows daily to avoid the heat of the desert.

But some lizards don't need legs. The California legless lizard moves like a snake—and even gets mistaken for a snake—as it slides through leaf litter searching for food. (Legless lizards have eyelids but snakes don't.)

brown basilisk/Jesus lizard

Scales & Tails

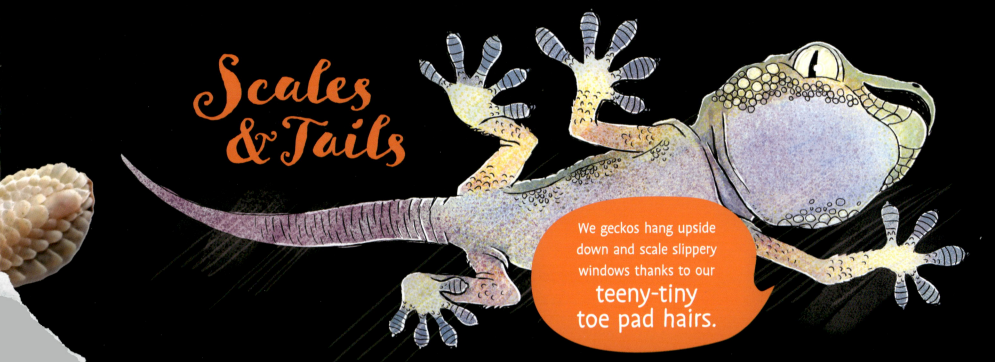

We geckos hang upside down and scale slippery windows thanks to our **teeny-tiny toe pad hairs.**

What's for DINNER?

Many lizards feast on insects. The chameleon sits and waits—searching as its eyes swivel in opposite directions. Once it finds its prey, the eyes focus together. Then…

FLICK! Lunch is served.

Other lizards are herbivores. Chuckwallas and rhinoceros iguanas eat leaves, flowers, and fruit.

Fierce-looking marine iguanas snack on seaweed in the ocean waters of the Galápagos Islands.

Komodo dragons aren't fussy. They dine on dead animals. They also hunt large prey like deer, wild boar, and water buffalo. Their venomous bites don't kill right away. Dragons wait for their prey to be weakened by blood loss before feasting.

juvenile veiled chameleon

Do lizards lay EGGS?

green iguana hatching from egg

five-lined skink hatchlings

Scales & Tails

Mama protected our nest, but now it's time to skedaddle! Those other Komodos think we're **dragon dinner.**

Male lizards show off when they feel threatened—or to attract a female. A push-up, head bob, dewlap display, or color change captures others' attention.

After mating, many lizards lay soft, leathery eggs. Some lay them in holes or grass. Others bury eggs in soil. Green iguanas lay more than fifty eggs, but many anoles lay just one.

Instead of laying eggs, sometimes a mother lizard keeps eggs inside her body until the little lizards hatch. Then she gives birth. Keeping eggs inside may help more babies survive harsh weather as well as predators. The greater short-horned lizard gives birth to hatchlings that weigh as little as a paper clip.

garden lizard covering eggs

How do LIZARDS GROW?

Madagascar day gecko molting

leopard gecko molting

Scales & Tails

Gross? Nah! Your skin sheds, too. My chunky skin pieces are just easier to see.

How about a skin sandwich?

Lizard skin is made of continuous scales formed from a tough material, much like our fingernails. It's called keratin. The scales and thick skin protect lizards from the sun and help them keep moisture inside their bodies. But lizard skin doesn't stretch.

As a lizard grows, its old skin gets too small. So, the skin sheds. New skin has already developed under the old skin. The skin falls off in big and small pieces. Many lizards even eat their old skin since it gives them important vitamins.

tokay gecko molting

adult male ambilobe panther chameleon

WHAT COLOR ARE LIZARDS?

male red-headed rainbow agama

southern tree agama

green iguana

Lizards come in a rainbow of colors. Chameleons and anoles are known for their bright colors. Male lizards often have bolder coloring than females. Typically, adults have brighter skin than young lizards.

Many species of lizards can change the color of their skin. Some lizards slightly adjust the color of their skin to be darker or lighter. But chameleons change dramatically from red to pink, green, yellow, and blue.

Scientists think lizards control their skin color based on temperature and mood. Lizards change color to camouflage with their environment and to communicate with other animals. Males' colorful changes say hello to females and tell others to back off.

veiled chameleon

ambilobe panther chameleon

Just call me Roy G. Biv. Or Rainbow Lizard. Or Red-Headed Rock Agama.

Scales & Tails

iguana under a rock

brown anole

wild northern spiny-tailed gecko

Mexican west coast giant horned lizard

regal horned lizard

Scales & Tails

My beaded lizard bite may not hurt much, but my venom will!

HOW DO LIZARDS PROTECT THEMSELVES?

Birds and snakes, meerkats and coyotes, scorpions and spiders, and even other lizards make meals out of lizards. So, these reptiles protect themselves in a variety of ways.

Most lizards are fast and flee to escape predators. Geckos and anoles often climb to safety. Chuckwallas scurry to rock crevices and then inflate their bodies so they can't be pulled from their hiding spot.

Some lizards sit still for hours and blend in with their environment. Color camouflage is especially important for slow movers like panther chameleons. Mossy leaf-tailed geckos hide in plain sight. They look like leaves.

Horned lizards defend themselves like no other. They take aim and fire—squirting blood from their eyes, which sends coyotes and wolves packing.

Blue tail skink

western green lizard

How Do Lizards use their TAILS?

Lizards use their tails to run, swim, and climb. Chameleon geckos even have a sticky tail tip that acts like a fifth foot.

Tails can even save lizards' lives. Special muscles let many lizards shed their tails to escape a predator. Some lizards lose their tails when something tugs on it. Others choose to drop their tails when threatened.

A bird approaches.

The lizard feels threatened and drops its tail.
Then the tail wiggles and wriggles for minutes, distracting the predator. The lizard scurries away with…

Scales & Tails

prehensile-tailed skink

THE FLICKING TONGUE.

THE COLOR-CHANGING SKIN.

THE WATCHFUL EYES.

And that's the truth about LIZARDS.

Pop! Off came my tail, but I'm not worried. I can grow a new one!

Can I have a pet Lizard?

Lizards can make great pets, but they aren't for everyone. Some lizards have big personalities and show interest in their humans—but not all of them. Are you thinking about a lizard pet? Their habitats need to be monitored closely and changed as needed, which makes them needy pets. Consider these questions and spend time learning more about lizard care.

Who will you choose?
Not all lizards make good pets. Some have many potential problems, while others, if cared for properly, can thrive in captivity. Learn with books and consult with an expert, if possible. Once you know your best lizard option, spend time really learning about the lizard's life in the wild and its needs as a pet.

Where will you keep the lizard?
Many lizards are small as juveniles and grow to great lengths—even bigger than you! Captive lizards—even small lizards—usually need a surprisingly large tank. Often lizards become highly stressed when sharing a habitat. Avoid sharing a home unless thorough research and expert consultations agree it's in the lizard's best interest.

Why do you want a lizard?
A lizard may be a great pet for you, but you may want to learn more before investing years as a lizard owner. Consider pet-sitting for others to gain experience and understand lizards' many needs better.

How much does a pet lizard cost?
The lizard itself can be affordable. However, it's important to understand that the proper tank with the necessary accessories to control temperature, humidity, and light can get quite expensive. Like with any pet, food must also be purchased regularly. (Consider how to store live insects if they are required for your lizard.)

What does the lizard need?
To help a lizard thrive as a pet, keep the tank habitat as close to nature as possible. It will need fresh water and food (possibly live insects). You will need to monitor and adjust the lighting, temperature, and humidity often. The lizard may also need perching or burrowing options.

When can you care for the lizard?
In addition to daily and weekly care, you also need to think about the future. Many lizards have long lives. Are you able to commit to lizard ownership for its entire life?

Scaly Superstars

leopard gecko

Flap-footed lizards jump with their long tails instead of feet to escape a predator.

Water anoles breathe underwater with the help of special skin.

Viviparous lizards live north of the Arctic Circle.

Northern spiny-tailed geckos squirt liquid from their tails as a defense.

Three-eyed lizards sense light changes and overhead predators with their third eyes.

Armadillo girdled lizards roll into tight balls to protect their underbelly.

Some **whiptail lizard** species reproduce with only females.

Panther chameleons grab prey that is 1/3 of their weight with their powerful tongues.

Marine iguanas drink so much saltwater they sneeze out salt.

Parachute geckos glide to safety from great heights.

Asian grass lizards have the longest of all animal tails (compared to the body lengths).

Gila monster venom is used to treat type 2 diabetes.

Terrific Tongue Test

A chameleon's tongue reaches for its prey. With precision and speed, the tongue stretches—and stretches and stretches some more. The sticky tip of the tongue, along with some natural suction, snatches the insect. The chameleon enjoys a tasty snack and waits for another critter to come near.

Test your "tongue" speed and accuracy with this challenge.

What You'll Need:

- party blower (also called a party horn)
- water
- cotton swab
- 10 or more bugs drawn on paper

What to Do:

1. Unroll the party horn.
2. Dip the cotton swab in water, and then wet the underside of the tip of the party horn.
3. Reroll the party horn.
4. Blow the horn and try to "eat" a bug. If a bug gets wet, it has been "eaten."
5. Moisten the party horn's tip as needed.
6. Repeat until all bugs are wet.
7. **Optional:** Challenge friends and see who can "eat" all the bugs the fastest.

29

frilled lizard

leaf-tailed gecko

secret toad-headed agama lizard

female Fischer's chameleon

Glossary

brumation: the state of reptile inactivity for an extended time, similar to hibernation

burrow: an underground home made from a tunnel

camouflage: the natural coloring of an animal that makes it hard to be seen

dewlap: loose skin on the throat of some animals

habitat: where a plant or animal usually lives

herbivore: an animal that eats only plants

hibernation: the state of deep sleep by an animal to survive winter

keratin: the hard protein fingernails, hair, and reptile scales are made from

predator: an animal hunting another animal for food

prey: the animal hunted by another animal for food

species: a group of animals that are the same type of animal

venom: the toxic substance injected with a bite or sting

vitamin: material found in food needed for health

Some Helpful Websites

animaldiversity.org

dkfindout.com/us

eol.org

reptile-database.org

These organizations dedicate themselves to herpetology (the study of reptiles and amphibians).

ssarherps.org

herpetologistsleague.org

Meet Annette Whipple

Annette Whipple celebrates curiosity and inspires others to live in wonder. She is the author of more than 20 fact-filled children's books including *The Laura Ingalls Wilder Companion: A Chapter-by-Chapter Guide*, *Quirky Critter Devotions*, and many animal books in The Truth About series. She's been named the 2025 Outstanding Pennsylvania Author by the Pennsylvania School Librarians Association. When Annette's not reading or writing, you might find her baking for her family or exploring a park near her home in Pennsylvania. Learn more about her and get a free teacher guide at her website.